# ABC LETTERS to Live By

## AN ALPHABET BOOK WITH INTENTION

Written by
**LISA FRENKEL RIDDIOUGH**

Illustrated by
**ÅSA GILLAND**

RP|KIDS
PHILADELPHIA

Running Press Kids
Hachette Book Group
1290 Avenue of the Americas, New York, NY 10104
www.runningpress.com/rpkids
@RP_Kids

Printed in China

First Edition: January 2022

Published by Running Press Kids, an imprint of Perseus Books, LLC,
a subsidiary of Hachette Book Group, Inc. The Running Press Kids name
and logo is a trademark of the Hachette Book Group.

The Hachette Speakers Bureau provides a wide range of authors for speaking events.
To find out more, go to www.hachettespeakersbureau.com or call (866) 376-6591.

The publisher is not responsible for websites (or their content)
that are not owned by the publisher.

Print book cover and interior design by Frances J. Soo Ping Chow

Library of Congress Cataloging-in-Publication Data
Names: Riddiough, Lisa Frenkel, author. | Gilland, Asa, illustrator.
Title: Letters to live by : an alphabet book with intention / written by Lisa Frenkel Riddiough;
illustrated by Asa Gilland. Description: First edition. | Philadelphia : RP Kids, 2022. |
Identifiers: LCCN 2021001013 (print) | LCCN 2021001014 (ebook) | ISBN 9780762473083
(hardcover) | ISBN 9780762473069 (ebook) | ISBN 9780762473212 (ebook)
Subjects: CYAC: Conduct of life—Fiction. | Alphabet. Classification: LCC PZ7.1.R535 Le 2022
(print) | LCC PZ7.1.R535 (ebook) | DDC [E]—dc23 LC record available at
https://lccn.loc.gov/2021001013 LC ebook record available at https://lccn.loc.gov/2021001014

978-0-7624-7308-3 (hardcover); 978-0-7624-7320-5 (ebook);
978-0-7624-7321-2 (ebook); 978-0-7624-7306-9 (ebook)

1010

10  9  8  7  6  5  4  3  2  1

For Mr. Greenebaum

—L.F.R.

To my first grade teacher
Marta W.

—Å.G.

# APPRECIATE ART

# BECOME BRAVE

CHOOSE COMPASSION

# DISCUSS DIFFERENCES

EMBRACE EDUCATION

FORGIVE FRIENDS

GIVE GENEROUSLY

# HAVE HEROES

INVITE IMAGINATION

KEEP KIND

LEARN LESSONS

# Move Mindfully

# Notice Neglect

OFFER OPTIONS

PRACTICE PEACE

# Quit Quarrelling

RESIST RUMORS

# SAVE SOMETHING

TAKE TIME

# UNTANGLE UNTRUTHS

# Value Volunteering

# WORK WILLINGLY

eXpect eXcellence

# YELL YES

Z'S THE DAY

We each have the power to make our world a better, happier place.
We all have the alphabet to guide us.

Which letters will you live by?

THE END